The Great Santa Kidnap

A Christmas Play

Roy Chatfield

A SAMUEL FRENCH ACTING EDITION

FOUNDED 1830

SAMUELFRENCH-LONDON.CO.UK
SAMUELFRENCH.COM

CHARACTERS

Fergus, Chief Forebrownie
Santa
Prancer, reindeer
Anna
Tommy
Snottle, goblin
Bug, goblin
Sneergripe, goblin
Granny Rabbit, rabbit
Colonel, sheep dog
Owl
Barbie, dragon
Sheep
Reindeer
Goblins

The action of the play takes place near the home of Anna and Tommy

Time: Christmas Eve

NOTES ON STAGING

The Prologue can be staged in front of the tabs, overflowing into the audience as necessary. Scene 1 is intended to follow on immediately.

Scene 2 opens in front of the tabs, which are opened as Anna and her companions go into the field.

In the second half, Scenes 3 and 5 use the full stage, while Scene 4 and the Epilogue are set in front of the tabs. Scene 4 should also use as much of the auditorium as possible.

If there is insufficient acting area in front of the tabs, the opening of the curtains in Scene 2 can be replaced by Colonel marching his sheep on stage. Similarly, in the Epilogue, the cast will need to enter rather than be revealed.

For the animals and goblins appropriate clothing, such as an officer's uniform for Colonel, together with face-paint and tail will be as effective as any more elaborate costume, and easier for the actors.

Santa's sleigh will have to be adapted to the turning area back stage. Its most important feature is the traces. The sleigh itself can be pared down to grips for Santa and Fergus. Where the theatre has suitable exit doors and sufficient space, it may be more convenient to use the area in front of the stage as the sleigh run.

Some of the references are topical to the time and place the play was written. Directors should feel free to substitute whatever is relevant to their particular audience.

R. C.

THE GREAT SANTA KIDNAP

Santa's Loading Bay

Brownies scuttle in and out, carrying boxes. Fergus enters with an extremely long list which he studies while giving orders to all and sundry that no-one takes any notice of

Fergus Hurry up, everybody, we haven't got all night! Collect the sacks for Canada and put them in bay forty-three! Someone call the store. We still need three hundred more cuddly yaks for Outer Mongolia! Make sure everything's in the right order, won't you? That's for bay three hundred and forty-one, then start loading the sacks for France! Don't forget we need four rubber palm trees this year! Have you got the Action Man Centre Forward for Manchester United? You haven't? Who's got it then? (*To the audience*) Any of you seen it? It must be somewhere.

A Brownie runs off with a piece of paper

Santa enters during the following

In Sack F four-seven-three-one. Why didn't you say so before? Get the doll's houses loaded next! (*To the audience*) It's always like this on Christmas Eve. One mad rush. Last minute orders coming in, toys to pack, the sleigh to load in exactly the right order to deliver everything without wasting time—do you know Santa and I have five hundred seventy-three million, one hundred seventy-six thousand, four hundred and ninety-two toys to deliver in one night? And the things some people want! It wouldn't be you that asked for an inflatable hamster, would it? Or a killer whale? Or a clockwork banana peeler? What did you ask for, then? I'll see what we can do. We sometimes make changes, though. Where we go first there's a know-all called Tommy who thinks he's getting twenty-three volumes of the *Encyclopaedia Britannica*. Well, he's not, he's getting a pair of football boots instead. Decisions,

decisions all the time. It's just as well I never panic. Cool, calm Fergus, that's me. I don't like to talk behind people's backs, but if it was left to Santa and the others—why, they'd miss out whole towns. Let's say you lived in Aardvarksdorp, South Africa, and your town wasn't here on the list. Imagine when you woke up on Christmas Day with no presents and... Tickling teeth, it isn't on the list! We've missed out Aardvarksdorp!

Santa Of course we haven't. (*He takes the list*) You're looking in the wrong place. Aardvark begins with two As.

Fergus That's a queer way of spelling anything. It's bound to give someone a nasty turn.

Santa It doesn't take much to put you in a tizzy. (*He continues to chat with the audience while Fergus becomes more and more impatient*) He's like this every year. Has he told you he runs my grotto all by himself? I thought he might have.

Fergus It's two minutes to midnight.

Santa So it is.

Fergus We'll never have the sleigh loaded in time.

Santa The Brownies finished loading it five minutes ago.

Fergus We should——

Santa We have.

Fergus Oh. We've still got the route to plan.

Santa Let's start at Winchester this year.

Fergus Last year you got lost round the one-way system.

Santa Timbuctu? Samboanga? Karabush? Andover? (*To the audience*) Where do you think we should go first? Right. Andover it is! Ah, here comes the reindeer.

Prancer and the reindeer enter with the sleigh

Prancer Ready to go, chief.

Fergus inspects the reindeer

Everything's ready. Don't fuss. (*To Santa*) Is he having another of his turns?

Fergus I've more sense than to trust you, Prancer.

The reindeer protest

Prancer You're jealous because Santa won't let you wear silver bells.
Santa Stop quarrelling, you two. It's almost Christmas Day and we've work to do.
Fergus (*looking hard at Prancer*) Some of us have already done some.

Santa and Fergus take their places on the sleigh

Santa Wait for the stroke of midnight.

Pause. A clock begins to strike

Christmas Day. Giddye, reindeer!

Reindeer exit with Santa and Fergus

SCENE 1

Outside Tommy and Anna's house

The clock continues to strike. The CURTAIN opens to reveal the outside of a house. Anna is looking out of a bedroom window

Anna It's Christmas Day, Tommy.
Tommy (*off*) No, it's not, it's the middle of the night.
Anna I heard the clock strike midnight.
Tommy (*off*) Don't wake me up when it strikes one.

Anna turns away

Snottle enters and dashes across the stage

Anna returns to the window

Snottle hides behind a dustbin

Anna I'm going to watch here all night.

Tommy appears at a window

Tommy Don't be dumb, Anna. What do you expect to see at this time of night?

Anna Santa, of course.

Tommy If he sees you looking out of the window, he won't come near our house, that's for sure.

Anna Don't you think so, Tommy?

Tommy Even Dracula wouldn't come near if he saw your face.

Anna thumps him

Snottle dashes off

Bug runs on and hides behind the dustbin

Anna I'm too excited to sleep. Don't you wonder what presents you'll find in the morning?

Tommy I already know.

Anna You would. You're that sort of brother. (*She mimics Tommy*) Don't you know this, Anna? Don't you know that, Anna? Oh, you are stupid, Anna!

Tommy You can't expect more than one clever person in every family. In our family, it's me.

Anna Rats! I bet you don't really know what you're getting.

Tommy The *Encyclopaedia Britannica.*

Bug I'm getting a train set.

Snottle (*off*) Be quiet.

Tommy I also know what you're going to get, Anna.

Anna Don't tell me.

Tommy leaves the window

Tommy! (*She turns*)

Bug exits

Sneergripe enters

Tommy appears at the window

Sneergripe hides behind the dustbin

You could whisper it.

Tommy Frostbite! Now, let's get some sleep. (*He draws the curtains*)

Sneergripe (*emerging from behind the dustbin*) I should think so, too. Don't children ever go to bed nowadays? When I was a young goblin, I had to be tucked in by eight o'clock sharp or else no bat droppings for breakfast. Let me introduce myself. Sneergripe's the name—master criminal and evil genius. Here, have one of my business cards. Any teachers anyone want sorted out? You, sir, you must know someone who should go for a swim with concrete boots on. My fees are very reasonable, I can assure you. Just leave your name and address at the box office, and I'll call round when I'm free. At the moment, though, I'm busy with a particularly dastardly crime, so you'll have to keep very quiet. Anyone who makes even the tiniest sound won't get any Christmas presents. Mind you, by the time I've finished, none of you are going to get any presents anyway.

Anna (*drawing back the curtain*) There's something in the garden. I bet it's a squirrel.

Sneergripe tries to act like a squirrel

Tommy (*off*) Don't be silly, Anna. Squirrels sleep all winter. It's probably a rabbit.

Sneergripe hops about

Or a cat.

Sneergripe (*becoming a cat*) Make up your mind, boy.

Anna It doesn't look like a cat.

Sneergripe Miaow! Miaow!

The noise of a window opening. A shoe hurtles towards Sneergripe

Voice (*off*) Shut your noise.

Sneergripe waves a fist back

Anna That's odd. The cat shook its fist at Mr Hopkins.

Tommy (*off*) Stop talking nonsense and go to sleep.

Anna draws the curtain

Sneergripe Pestiferous child.

The heads of Snottle and Bug appear

Snottle Is it safe to come out now?
Bug Can I play squirrels now, Sneergripe? Or dogs? I can do a super howl. (*He demonstrates a howl*)

Snottle quickly stops him

Sneergripe Now Bug has stopped pretending to be the whole of Noah's Ark, can we turn to tonight's business, which is flying reindeer.
Bug I can't do one of them.
Sneergripe Be quiet, Bug. Now, Snottle, you remember what I was saying about flying reindeer.
Snottle They fly.
Sneergripe Of course they fly, you broomhead. What do they eat?

Bug produces a tennis ball, and practises dribbling with it

Snottle I've never tried keeping one.
Sneergripe ⎱ (*together*) ⎰ Cabbage and cold porridge.
Bug ⎰   ⎱ What a goal!
Sneergripe We are trying to be quiet!
Bug (*picking up the ball*) Sorry, Sneergripe.

Anna appears at the window

The goblins group together, pretending to be a bush

Anna Tommy, did we have a bush in our garden yesterday? (*She looks back at Tommy*)

The three goblins scatter

Tommy (*off*) No, and we haven't got one today.
Anna (*rubbing her eyes*) Maybe I am tired, after all. (*She closes the curtains*)

The goblins enter

Sneergripe As I was saying before Bug woke up half the neighbourhood, flying reindeer eat cabbage and cold porridge.

Snottle They must be mad.

Sneergripe That may be so, but they like it so much they can smell it from ten miles away. And once they do smell it, nothing will stop them following the scent.

Bug Can I go home now? I'm cold.

Sneergripe No, you're needed here.

Bug I'm hungry.

Sneergripe Go and nick some sweets then.

Bug (*to the audience*) Anyone with choccies, sweets and any other goodies, hand over. Except aniseed balls. I don't like them. What you got there? They're not aniseed balls, are they? (*He argues about this with the audience*)

Sneergripe If you're going to nick them, nick them. Don't make a speech about it.

Bug I've got to find out if they're aniseed balls, haven't I?

Sneergripe Find out quietly.

During the following lines Bug tries to mime "Are these sweets aniseed balls? If not, I'm taking them."

Snottle I think we'd be better off without Bug. He's as thick as two planks.

Sneergripe Firstly, you don't think, Snottle, that's your trouble.

Snottle Sorry, Sneergripe.

Sneergripe Secondly, you underestimate dear Bug. He's as thick as four planks. Thirdly, we are about to commit a fiendish and daring crime. We need someone to do the dangerous bit.

Snottle We need someone brave for that.

Sneergripe Give me the name of one brave goblin.

Snottle Er...

Sneergripe Exactly. Since we don't have a hero available, we need someone so stupid he doesn't know he's being brave. (*He claps Bug on the back*) Someone like our good friend Bug.

Bug What does fiendish mean?

Sneergripe Shut up, Bug, and fetch the box.

Bug exits

Er, Snottle... There might be a little bit of money coming in from this. The odd pound or two maybe. We don't want to worry Bug about that, do we?

Snottle You mean we keep it all ourselves.

Bug enters with a large box

Sneergripe Open it up, Bug.

Bug does so

What does it say?
Bug This way up.
Sneergripe Not what it says on the outside, stupid. What does it say inside?
Bug "Grandma Grumble's Olde English Cabbage and Cold Porridge Cookies". Best before the first of January. Made in Hong Kong.
Sneergripe We have here twenty-four packets of cabbage and cold porridge cookies.
Bug We've only got six days to eat them.
Sneergripe Firstly, Bug, there are seven days left, and secondly, we don't eat them ourselves. We leave them out for the nice reindeer who'll soon be passing this way.
Snottle I know you'll call me stupid, Sneergripe, but we goblins are evil and wicked and all that. We ought to be causing havoc, not feeding hungry reindeer. I mean, they like this muck, don't they?
Sneergripe I'm not going to call you stupid, Snottle. I'll call you a brainless, block-headed, bumblepuff instead. What's the date?
Snottle I don't know. Bug ate the calendar, didn't he?
Sneergripe It's Christmas, Snottle, Christmas. What does that remind you of?
Bug Christmas pud.
Snottle Holly.
Bug Mince pies.
Snottle The Queen on telly.
Bug Being sick behind the Christmas tree.
Snottle Aunt Edna's hand-knitted socks.
Bug Lots of prezzies.
Snottle ⎱ *(together) Santa Claus!*
Bug ⎰
Sneergripe Exactly. Tonight, gentlemen, we will kidnap Santa Claus.
Bug *(worried)* Does that mean I won't get my present?

Scene 1

The sound of bells, approaching

Sneergripe We'll get our presents, Bug. No-one else will, but we'll be all
right. Now listen. When you hear sleigh bells——
Bug What do they sound like?
Snottle You hear those bells now? Like that.
Sneergripe Santa's coming! Don't just stand there. Bug, empty some of
those cookies on the ground. When the reindeer start eating them, run
out and cut their traces.
Snottle He means the leather bits.
Sneergripe Snottle, jump Santa from behind and tie him up. No granny
knots, mind.
Snottle What will you be doing?
Sneergripe Keeping watch from behind this dustbin. (*Challengingly*) We
can't all have the chance to be heroes, can we? Come on now, move!

Bug scatters the cookies. The goblins hide

The sleigh enters, with the reindeer intent on the cookies

Santa Whoa, whoa. No time for eating now.
Prancer Just a quick bite, Santa.
Fergus I'll give you a quick bite if you don't get going.
Prancer Misery!

Bug leaps out. He jostles with the reindeer

Snottle pulls Fergus into the empty box

The sleigh exits, with Bug still among the reindeer

Snottle I've got him! I've got him!
Sneergripe (*appearing from behind the dustbin*) I'm rich, I'm rich, I'm
really rich! (*He links hands with Snottle and dances round Fergus*)
Where's Bug gone?
Snottle I expect he's nicking some more sweets.
Sneergripe Just when we need him to carry Santa. Do I have to do
everything myself? (*He pauses*) Well, what are you waiting for? Pick
him up.

Snottle tries to pick Fergus up with no success. Next he tries pulling him along by the legs. He leans back too far and falls over on top of the dustbin

Anna and Tommy appear in the window

Anna What's happening?
Sneergripe Dustmen, luv.

Snottle straightens up

Tommy In the middle of the night?
Snottle You don't expect us to come on Christmas Day, do you?
Anna But you came this morning as well.
Sneergripe Of course. It's Christmas, isn't it? Everyone gets something extra, don't they? Last Christmas the council sent everybody an extra council tax demand. This time it's an extra bin collection.
Tommy They're making so much noise, they must be dustmen. (*He pulls Anna away from the window*)
Sneergripe Can't a goblin carry out an honest kidnapping without those brats poking their nose in every five minutes. Hurry up, Snottle, and no more noise.
Snottle Can't you take one leg as well, Sneergripe?
Sneergripe Oh, all right. (*He seizes one of Fergus's legs*) Here, this leg is brown. Santa's legs are red.
Snottle Perhaps he's cold.
Sneergripe Let's have a look at him.

Snottle takes off the box

Fergus What is the meaning of this outrage!
Sneergripe Stop moaning and tell us your name.
Fergus I am Fergus Lebrun, Chief fore——
Sneergripe Shove him back.

Snottle shoves him back

   You've got the wrong one, you nurdle.
Snottle We could sell him down the market. Get a bob or two that way?
Sneergripe Quiet, I'm thinking.
Snottle Don't think too long. The sleigh's coming back. (*He tries to leave*)

Sneergripe You're not going anywhere. Shove this one in the bin and try again. (*He hides*)

Bug enters, chased by the reindeer and Santa

Santa Stop thief!
Bug Not likely.
Prancer Grab him, lads.

Snottle grabs Santa

Bug and the sleigh exit

Snottle Gotcha.
Sneergripe (*emerging to inspect the new captive*) This one looks more like Santa. Box him up and get moving.

Snottle gags Santa and puts him in the box

Snottle What about Bug?
Sneergripe I don't suppose the reindeer will do him too much harm.
Snottle Goodbye, Bug. Hey, he's coming back this way. Mind that lamppost.

A crash off stage

He's snapped it in two.
Sneergripe He always was a strong lad.

Bug enters, pummelled by the reindeer

Bug Help, Mother!
Prancer Hand back Fergus or we'll bite your knees off.

Bug and the reindeer exit

There is a second, louder crash

Snottle Slap bang into a brick wall.
Sneergripe Scatter some more cookies, quick.

They do so at every exit

The reindeer drift back on stage and exit in all directions, munching as they go

Come on, Bug, there's no time to take a rest.

Bug staggers on

Bug Someone put a wall in the way.
Sneergripe Never mind about that. Stick this notice on the sleigh.

Bug exits

He doesn't look well.
Snottle The wall looks worse.

Bug enters

Sneergripe Help Snottle carry Santa. And bring the rest of those cookies. They might come in useful when we kidnap Lady Di.

They exit singing "We're rich", etc.

Anna appears at the window

Anna The dustmen are chasing that poor cat. Stop it at once!

Prancer enters in search of more cookies

Prancer Stop what?
Anna It's a reindeer! A real reindeer. Tommy, wake up!
Tommy (*off*) I haven't had a chance to get to sleep yet.
Anna There's a reindeer in our garden.

Tommy comes to the window

Tommy Don't be an idiot, Anna. The only place you'll see a reindeer in this country is a zoo. You probably saw—Hell's teeth—reindeer!

Anna rushes off

Anna (*off*) Mum! Dad! Wake up, I've seen a reindeer.

Tommy They'll kill her. They'll surely kill her.

Prancer (*to the audience*) Do British children always behave in this extraordinary way? What does she expect to see on Christmas day—a brontosaurus?

Tommy (*to Anna*) What did they say?

Anna Mum said "Go away" and Dad said "Scram or I'll wring your neck". What shall we do now?

Tommy Go back to bed.

Anna You can if you like. I'm going to have a closer look.

She leaves the window

Tommy Don't you dare. It's long past midnight. (*He pauses*) Sisters!

Anna comes out of the house pulling on a sweater

Anna Wow! (*She pulls on her wellies*)

Tommy comes out of the house, still dressing himself

Tommy You're useless, Anna, you really are. Don't you realise it's about fifty degrees below zero out here?

Anna But isn't he beautiful? (*She moves towards Prancer*)

Tommy (*pulling her back*) If I wasn't here to look after you, I don't know what might happen. Don't you realise reindeer have sharp teeth, sharp horns——

Prancer Antlers.

Tommy (*not noticing where the correction came from*) Antlers, and can kick like Gary Lineker?

Anna Don't be silly, Tommy. He won't do me any harm. He's a Christmas reindeer.

Prancer That's right. (*He preens*) Ordinary reindeer don't have such elegant legs.

Tommy Anna—am I imagining things or did——

Prancer Speak? Of course I did. Most animals can if only you humans would find something sensible to ask them. "Pussy like nice drink?" doesn't set the brain cells racing, you know.

Anna Tommy never asks questions. He only answers them.

Prancer I rather thought he was a pain in the fetlock.

Anna Are you one of Santa's reindeer?

Prancer A bit more than that. I'm Prancer, the team leader. Just look at my harness. Isn't it fine? The bells are real silver, of course. Nothing but the best for Santa's reindeer.

Tommy (*rudely*) Then why aren't you pulling a sleigh?

Prancer (*embarrassed*) Ah, yes, well. You could say things haven't gone quite according to plan.

Anna What happened?

Prancer We were ambushed by goblins. Our traces were cut, my team of reindeer scattered and Santa—gone.

Tommy You've certainly got problems.

Prancer No, Tommy, you've got the problems. If we don't find Santa, you'll get no Christmas present.

Tommy No *Encyclopaedia Britannica*!

Prancer (*to the audience*) I might have known it was him.

Anna Shouldn't we be doing something to find him?

Tommy Of course we should. Prancer, you go and find the other witnesses. Anna, you look for clues here. I'll go and examine the sleigh. We'll soon crack this case.

He exits towards the sleigh

Prancer Witnesses? What is he on about? There were only us reindeer and we were too busy eating to see... I don't mean eating, I mean... I don't know what I mean, but I didn't see anything.

Anna Tommy knows all about this sort of thing. He reads books and guesses who the murderer is.

Prancer Murderer! Don't say that!

Anna Please, Prancer, find the other reindeer like Tommy said. He does know what he's talking about—well, sometimes he does.

Prancer That's easy. See this whistle? (*He blows it*) While we're waiting, let's look for the clues.

They wander round studying the ground

Anna (*seeing Fergus in the bin*) This sack isn't yours, is it?

Prancer The legs look familiar.

Anna (*pulling Fergus out*) I knew they weren't real dustmen.
Fergus You're not Santa. Explain yourself.

During the next few exchanges, the reindeer enter one by one

Anna I'm Anna Upwood.
Prancer She's helping us find Santa.
Fergus Find? You've not gone and lost Santa on Christmas night, have you?

Tommy enters carrying a scrap of paper

Tommy I've found a note pinned on the back of the sleigh.
Anna What does it say?
Tommy "We have Santa. If you want him back, pay six million pounds cash in used notes into the Goblin Bank, Crimes Account. No cash, no more Santa. Merry Christmas from the Syndicate." Then there's a PS: "And a train set as well. Love, Bug."
Fergus Kidnappers on Christmas night! We don't have time to waste on such nonsense. Tell them to give Santa back right away. (*To the reindeer*) Well, go on.
Prancer Who are we going to tell?
Fergus The kidnappers, of course.
Prancer But we don't know who they are.
Fergus Then find out.
Prancer Who do you think I am, Sherlock Holmes with antlers?
Fergus No, you're just a gobbling reindeer who can't think further than cabbage and cold porridge cookies. (*To Tommy and Anna*) That's how it was done. The kidnappers laid a trail of the stuff. Down flew lots of greedy reindeer to eat it all up. Smell it for miles, they can. (*To the reindeer*) And while they went munch, they lost Santa, didn't they?
Prancer We chased the kidnapper. What did you do?
Fergus I was kidnapped too, wasn't I?
Prancer Threw you back pretty quick, didn't they?
Tommy Which way did the kidnappers go?
Reindeer (*pointing in different directions*) That way!
Fergus Typical! (*To the audience*) Which way was it?

The audience tells him

Then which way—right, left, or straight on?

Pause

Nobody knows.

Tommy We need a tracker dog.

Fergus We also need Santa. Instead we've got nine useless reindeer.

Anna Do you think the kidnappers had any of those cabbage and cold porridge things left?

Tommy This is no time to be hungry, Anna.

Anna I was only thinking that if the kidnappers did still have some, and if the reindeer could really smell it for miles...

Prancer We can do that all right.

Anna You could lead us right to their front door.

Fergus Brilliant! Prancer, you can make yourself useful for once. The rest of you, get that sleigh repaired. We'll have to shift some once we get Santa back. But that won't take long, not now it won't.

Tommy Back to bed.

Anna Not likely. I'm not going to miss out on this.

Tommy Another fine mess you're getting us into. Don't say I didn't warn you, that's all.

Everyone exits

The Lights fade out

Scene 2

A footpath

Sneergripe enters, followed at a distance by Snottle and Bug, carrying Santa in the box

Sneergripe Get a move on, we're supposed to be making a getaway, not taking a stroll.

Snottle It's Bug's fault. He keeps falling over.

Bug A tree tripped me up, didn't it?

Snottle He's dropped the cookies in the stream.

Sneergripe You've done what?

Bug There was this tree root across the path, and next minute I was on the path with it.

Sneergripe You had no business to be. Those cookies didn't come from Tesco at fifty pence a packet, you know. They cost an arm and a leg, as you'll find out when I deduct it from your pocket money.

Bug You never give me any.

Sneergripe That's beside the point. Now come on, can't you?

They drop the box on the ground

Snottle Can't the prisoner walk? He weighs a ton.

Sneergripe A bit of weightlifting will get you fit, Snottle; build you up into a healthy goblin.

He exits

Snottle It's all right for Sneergripe, he's not carrying him.

They pick up the box with Santa and set off. Bug slips and both fall down

Must you find every bit of mud? Let's have a breather anyway.

Snottle stretches out. Bug walks round trying to keep warm. Eventually he tries doing exercises

Don't do that, it makes me feel tired watching you.

Bug I'm in training for the big match, aren't I?

Snottle You don't need to do exercises for that. You're always sent off after five minutes for kicking the ref.

Bug That's what I mean. I want to cut it down to three minutes. (*He sits down and pulls out a football comic*)

Snottle (*after a pause*) I still don't see why we have to carry him. He's got legs, hasn't he?

Bug tips Santa out of the box and ungags him

Bug Have you any legs?

Santa *Help!*

Bug claps a hand round his mouth

Snottle Tell him one more squeak, and you'll break every bone in his body.

Bug One more squeak and you'll break every bone in his body. (*He releases his grip*)

Santa You realise you're spoiling everyone's Christmas.

Snottle You won't spoil ours once we get the ransom... The train set for Bug.

Bug One that goes chuff.

Santa And how, may I ask, am I expected to deliver a train set when I'm lying tied up on a path in the middle of nowhere?

Bug I don't know. You'll have to ask Sneergripe. He's good at questions like that.

Santa The answer is, I can't.

Pause

Which is a pity, when you come to think of it. There's a really super train set at my Greenland factory. Three locomotives, sixteen coaches, Pullman car, mail van, goods trucks—everything you need.

Bug As long as it goes chuff.

Santa It does everything except make tea. It does clickety-clack, clickety-clack.

Bug Clickety-clack, clickety-clack. Chuff chuff.

Santa demonstrates its range of sounds, with Bug copying him

Santa Pity you can't have it, isn't it?

Bug Who says I can't?

Santa Well, I'm here and it's there.

Bug Oh.

Santa (*after a pause*) I could go and fetch it, I suppose.

Bug Let's!

Santa Strangers aren't allowed at Greenland Headquarters. You'll have to wait here. Promise you won't go away.

Bug I promise.

Santa Let me go then.

Bug (*halfway through untying him*) Just a mo'; you might not come back.

Santa I'll come back, I promise you. And I'll bring the train set. Plus all my Brownies with a few other things.

Bug Like what?

Santa That would spoil the surprise.

Bug I won't let you go if you don't tell.

Santa All right. Clubs, swords, guns, panda cars, half the Hampshire police force—that sort of thing.

Bug All for me.

Santa You'll have to share them with your two friends. The policemen would like that.

Bug (*finishing untying him*) Don't be too long.

Santa runs out

Snottle looks up

Snottle Where's the prisoner?

Bug Gone to get my train set.

Snottle (*leaping up*) He's escaping, you fool. If we don't get him back, Sneergripe will kill us.

Bug and Snottle run after Santa

There is a commotion off stage, then silence

The goblins return, dragging Santa with them

Santa I was only getting a train set for your friend.

Snottle Any more tricks like that and you'll get thumped. Shove him in the box again, Bug.

Santa is trussed up. Bug tries to put him back in the box

Bug He won't go in.

Snottle He came out all right. (*He tries without success*) I dunno. It's a puzzle, isn't it?

Granny Rabbit enters. She stands behind Snottle watching them struggle

Granny I'd put the head in first, if I were you.

Snottle (*turning round*) What do you want?

Granny I like to know what's going on in the world.

Snottle Try reading a newspaper.

Bug and Snottle try yet again to pack Santa. Santa tries to wriggle free

Maybe we should try shoving his head in first.
Granny Wrapping a present, are we?
Snottle What do you think we're doing?
Granny Kidnapping Santa Claus.

Bug and Snottle leap up

Bug (*menacingly*) You said something?
Granny Really, you goblins! Can't take a joke, can you? (*She moves away in a huff, but a thought strikes her. She turns*) Silly me! That was your joke, wasn't it?
Bug (*asking Snottle*) Was it?
Snottle (*to Bug*) If it gets rid of the old coot it was.
Granny (*looking more closely*) You must admit it does look like Santa.
Snottle It's a model Santa. Made in Japan.

Santa makes a dash for freedom, but Bug is too quick

Santa Help! Get the police.
Granny What a strange thing to say.
Snottle Japanese, isn't it?
Santa Thieves! Kidnappers!
Snottle Switch him off, Bug.
Bug Do what?
Snottle Sit on his head. (*To Granny*) They do the switches in funny places sometimes, don't they?
Granny There's something odd going on here. He distinctly said kidnappers.
Snottle It sounded like that, yes, but what he really said was "Ki-Na-Po". It's Japanese for—ur—what's it Japanese for, Bug?
Bug Shut up or you get thumped.
Granny They do make violent toys nowadays, don't they? I don't think you can beat a traditional present. Like carrots! Want one?
Bug Love one. (*He takes one*)
Santa Madam, I really am Santa.

Snottle Give him a carrot too.

Bug stuffs a carrot in Santa's mouth

Snottle Smart, these Japanese. You don't find many robots that eat carrots.

Granny I think there's something odd going on here. He's too real looking to be a robot. (*She looks closer*) Why, I do believe he's breathing.

Bug He won't be much longer if he don't keep his mouth shut.

Granny Are you telling Granny Rabbit the truth?

Snottle ⎱ (*together*) ⎰ Yes.
Bug ⎰   ⎱ No.

Santa ⎱   ⎰ (*spitting out the carrot*) They're telling you a
          ⎰ (*together*) ⎰ pack of lies. I'm Santa, not a Japanese robot.
Snottle ⎰   ⎱ Stuff another carrot in his mouth.

Bug takes the carrot from Granny

Granny (*snatching the carrot back*) None of your Goblin ways with me, my lad. (*To Snottle*) Explain this, then. If he's a Christmas present, why aren't you using wrapping paper?

Bug He wouldn't be able to breathe, would he? I mean, all that paper round his mouth.

Snottle Hasn't he got a sense of humour? He makes me laugh so much I could strangle him.

Granny I think the police should be told about this.

Bug Why?

Granny You're kidnapping a Japanese robot, aren't you?

Snottle takes one arm, Bug the other

Snottle You can't kidnap a robot.

Granny You can't?

Bug No, you can nick 'em, but you can't kidnap 'em.

Snottle So why don't you go quietly home and wrap up your nice carrots in some nice wrapping paper.

Granny Wrapping paper! Do you know, I've left it behind at Uncle Fred's. I must fly.

She exits

Snottle Right, let's try again.

Granny pops her head on stage

Granny Those people coming now might help you with the parcel.

She exits

Snottle Good, we need a hand.

Pause

Here, what people?

Bug goes to look

Bug It's only someone falling over the same tree root as me.
Snottle It's the fuzz, you fool. Pick up that end and run.

Bug and Snottle hurry off with Santa; Bug re-enters to pick up the box

Bug (*to the audience*) Must go. Leave some of your sweeties for me,
won't you?

Snottle sticks his head in from the wings

Snottle And if they ask, we went that way. Got it?

Bug and Snottle exit, leaving Bug's comic behind

Prancer, Tommy, Anna and Fergus enter

Prancer What a waste! All those cabbage and cold porridge cookies just
thrown into the stream.
Anna I'm sure they didn't mean to do it. I bet whoever was carrying them
tripped over that tree root like Tommy did.
Tommy I didn't fall over anything. I bent to look for footprints.

Anna Flat on your face in the mud.

Tommy Whose fault is it that we're here in the first place?

Anna No-one asked you to come. I can manage quite well by myself, thank you, without big brother trotting along behind.

Tommy Don't get big-headed because you had one bright idea. You're not due to get another for at least ten years.

Anna OK, clever dick, tell us what happens now.

Fergus That's simple enough. The trail's gone cold. There's no scent for Prancer to follow anymore, so we're stuck.

Prancer I could take another look at the packets in the water. Some of them might be only a little bit wet.

Fergus Can't you stop thinking about your tum for five minutes? If we don't find Santa—I can't bear to think about what will happen.

Tommy No more presents.

Fergus Worse than that, much worse. There's more to Christmas than presents, you know. I'll tell you a secret. Santa's real job isn't to hand out lots of gifts—anyone can do that. It's to make sure everyone has Christmas joy. Frankly, the presents are a bit of a nuisance.

Anna Then why give any?

Fergus Because you humans never appreciate anything you can't see. But if there wasn't any joy in the presents, you'd soon notice something wrong.

Anna Then we've got to find Santa.

Fergus How? That's the point.

Anna Can't we...? You read the books, Tommy, make yourself useful for once.

Tommy We should scout around for footprints—or bits of cloth caught in the hedge. That's another good clue.

Fergus Goblins have hooves with two toes. One big, one little.

Tommy It hasn't rained for a day or two, so there's not much mud left on this path.

Prancer I'll go and look by the stream. There's plenty of mud there.

Fergus No. Tommy will do that. You go that way where there are no cookies to distract you. If you take this part of the path, Anna, I'll take the other. Everyone know what we're looking for?

They exit in different directions

Anna is alone. She searches the stage until she finds the comic

Anna Tommy, Fergus, I've found something.

Tommy enters

Tommy Where?
Anna There's a football magazine there.
Tommy (*picking it up*) I've read that one.
Anna Isn't it a clue?
Tommy Goblins don't play football. Is that all you've found?

Fergus and Prancer enter

Anna No, look at the patch of mud by the gate here.
Fergus That's a goblin print all right. The point is, which direction is he going?
Prancer And is it the right goblin?
Fergus Don't make difficulties.
Anna There's a gate here.
Prancer And a stile along there.
Fergus And another along here.
Tommy Or they could have kept to this path.

They try to puzzle this out

Prancer Shall I call the others?
Fergus Without wishing to be rude, Prancer, one reindeer is enough for me to cope with in a crisis.
Tommy I think this is a decoy. They want us to think they've left this path, but really, they haven't.
Prancer Obviously they were going to the stile along here. (*He points right*)
Fergus You don't know anything about it. Goblins always go left, so they'll take that stile. (*He points left*)
Prancer Why?
Fergus Because it's on their left, nitwit.
Tommy That would depend which way they were facing.
Anna They could have been facing any direction, so we're no further forward.
Prancer (*to the audience*) You've been quiet. Did you see which way they went? You did?

The audience says yes

Fergus How many?

The audience tells him

Prancer Too many.
Fergus Which way did they go?

The audience tells him

That's decided then. We go left like I said.
Colonel (*off*) Have you no brains?
Fergus Who said that?

Colonel enters

Colonel Not a brain among you.
Anna (*indicating the gate*) There's someone in that field.
Fergus Battle stations everyone. (*To Prancer*) And don't you dare ring even one tiny bell.
Prancer Don't worry. I'll keep well out of the way.
Fergus Now you keep that side, Anna, and you, Tommy—you'd best be there. Now open the gate and surprise them!

The Curtain *opens to reveal Colonel trying to drill the Sheep*

Colonel Keep in line! In line, I said. Don't you know what a line is?
Sheep No, sir.
Colonel My brass buttons! How can anyone expect me to turn you into a proper flock? If I added all your brains together there wouldn't be enough to make a gnat's finger. You know what a gnat is, don't you?
Sheep Yes, sir.
Colonel You do?
Sheep Er—no.
Fergus (*stepping forward*) Ahem.

Colonel whirls round. Fergus bows

Fergus Lebrun, Chief Forebrownie to His Jolliness Santa Claus.

Colonel (*saluting*) Colonel Canine, Commander-in-Chief, Dingle Farm
foot regiment of sheep at your service.

Anna Why are all the sheep in a line?

Colonel A line you call it, eh? I'd call it a shambles. But that doesn't
answer your questions, ma'am. And maybe I shouldn't.

Anna Why not?

Colonel Top secret, don't you know?

Anna I didn't mean to——

Tommy She's nosey, that's all.

Anna Tommy!

Colonel No offence taken, ma'am. And if you promise not to breathe a
word...

Anna We promise, don't we, Tommy?

Tommy I'm certainly not going to tell anybody about talking sheep—I'd
never live it down.

Colonel What you see here is training for next year's sheep dog trials. By
next summer these sheep must be able to start in a neat flock, march
abreast for fifty yards, then reform inside a sheep pen. I'll be watching
them like a hawk while they do it, I can promise. They'll run riot
otherwise—stealing the cream buns, biting the vicar. Really, they've
got no more discipline than a flock of sheep.

Anna But they are sheep.

Colonel Well, yes, they are, but even so. You just watch a little and you'll
soon see. Now, sheep, let's find out if you're anything more than
walking wool blankets. Atten—shun!

The sheep try to form a straight line without much success

From the right, number off! Don't tell me. You don't know which side
is right. You there, you start.

Sheep 1 Bah.

Sheep 2 Bah.

Sheep 3 Bah.

Sheep 4 Bah.

Sheep 5 Moo.

Colonel Moo? What do you mean, moo?

Sheep 5 Oh, do I mean meow? Er—I know. Woof.

Colonel My brass buttons! Why don't you go cock-a-doodle-doo while
you're at it?

Sheep 5 Cock-a-doodle-doo.

Colonel Bah! Bah! Can't you go bah like any normal sheep? You... You... You overgrown pillow you. (*To Anna*) Sometimes, ma'am, I despair.

Anna Don't do that, please.

Colonel Every year we win something. Three years running a blue ribbon and a juicy bone. Next year—nothing. Not unless fluff-brain there wins the dog show. (*To the sheep*) Woof! I'll woof you, my lad.

Anna I bet all the other flocks are even worse.

Colonel Now you come to mention it, ma'am, that's more than likely. Why, Major Bob over at Derrydown Farm has a flock that makes strong dogs weep. Do you know, at the last show——

Fergus This is all very interesting, I'm sure, but it's one o'clock on Christmas morning and we still have no Santa.

Colonel I say, old man, that's serious.

Fergus Colonel, it is worse than serious. I suppose you wouldn't have seen a goblin or two pass this way carrying anything Santa-shaped?

Colonel Goblins, eh? Can't say I have.

Tommy Didn't I say it was a decoy?

Colonel But if it's a goblin you're looking for?

Fergus There's no doubt about that.

Colonel Then your best bet would be the Goblin Hollows. Keep walking this way and you'll come to a large wood.

Tommy I know where you mean.

Colonel Right in its heart there's a circle of dead trees. You know that as well?

Tommy Dead Man's Ditch.

Colonel That's where you'll find the Goblin Hollows.

Tommy But I've been there lots of times.

Colonel Not looking for goblins, though, I'll be bound. Nor, I think, after dark. You'll find the wood is different at night. As for Dead Man's Ditch—well, I wouldn't go there in a hurry, not after dark.

Fergus We haven't much choice. Come on, every one.

Anna Thanks, Colonel.

Colonel Thank you, ma'am, for cheering me up.

Fergus, Tommy, Anna and Prancer exit

Don't forget your promise about military secrets. And good luck! (*He*

pauses) I'm afraid you'll need it. (*He pauses*) Ah, well, back to work.
Sheep, form a line!

As the sheep try yet again to form a straight line——

——the CURTAIN *falls*

SCENE 3

Dead Man's Ditch

*Sneergripe enters, followed by Snottle and Bug carrying Santa. He
unlocks the door in a tree trunk*

Sneergripe Dump him in the dungeon, lads. Bug, you'll have to stand
guard down there.
Bug Can't I have a snooze?
Sneergripe Not after dropping the cookies in the stream, you can't. I had
plans for them, I did.
Bug I brought back the box, didn't I?
Sneergripe As I recall, the last time I saw that box it had Santa in it. Would
someone care to explain how you lost him?
Snottle Bug did it.
Bug There was this train, see, and——
Sneergripe The dungeon, Bug, and no sleeping on duty.
Snottle Look on the bright side, Bug. I can have a sleep instead.

Bug and Snottle take Santa inside

Sneergripe (*to the audience*) That's that, then. All I have to do now is sit
back and wait for six million quid to roll in. Dead easy, isn't it? Mind
you, you haven't seen anything yet. See this list? Anyone worth
kidnapping is on it. (*He flicks through several sheets of paper*) Let's see.
Ah, Lady Di. Now, she must be worth four million pounds to someone.
And Fergie—there's another four million. Mrs Thatcher—anyone give
me four million for her? All right, then. Ten pence. You look about the
right size for this stupid bag. (*To someone in the audience*) Would you
like to be kidnapped? (*To their companion*) You'd give me a couple of

pounds to get him back, wouldn't you? OK, tell you what, you give me a fiver to hang on to him. (*He pulls out a notebook*) Add five pounds to the total, divide by one, and... (*He counts on his fingers*) That'll be enough. I'm saving up to buy Australia, you see. I've always fancied owning a continent. Sneergripia would sound so much nicer than Australia, don't you think? Imagine the headlines in the papers— Sneergripia wins the Ashes, Sneergripia wins the Davis Cup, Sneergripia wins the America Cup. It'd better win them, otherwise I'll send Bug out to nick them.

Snottle enters

Snottle I've given Bug the cutlass and the blunderbuss.
Sneergripe Was that wise, Snottle? Last time he shot a hole in the ceiling.
Snottle I didn't give him any gunpowder.
Sneergripe You did right.
Snottle The dragon wants to know if there'll be brandy butter with the bread and water, it being Christmas and that.
Sneergripe We're running a dungeon, not a hotel. Tell him to get lost.
Snottle There was one other little thing.
Sneergripe Well?
Snottle I was sort of thinking.
Sneergripe I doubt it, but go on.
Snottle When we get paid, we let Santa go, right? So he'll go straight to the police.
Sneergripe So what?
Snottle They'll come round and arrest us, won't they? Then what will happen?
Sneergripe They'll charge you with kidnapping, assault, stealing, dangerous driving, damaging council property, cruelty to reindeer, leaving litter and causing general misery. I'd reckon thirty years hard labour for that lot. Forty if the judge didn't like you. I don't suppose he will, somehow.
Snottle They can't put us in jail for forty years!
Sneergripe Not us, Snottle. Only you and Bug.
Snottle You were there too.
Sneergripe Maybe, but I didn't do anything, did I?
Snottle Forty years!
Sneergripe *C'est la vie*, as they say in Germany. However...

Snottle Yes?

Sneergripe I've still got plenty of work for you to do, so I can't have you sneaking off to jail yet awhile.

Snottle Thanks, Sneergripe.

Sneergripe So we don't let Santa go.

Snottle Not take the ransom money?

Sneergripe Of course we take it. I didn't carry him all this way for nothing, did I?

Snottle But we can't take the money and not give him back. That wouldn't be honest.

Sneergripe Snottle, you bore me. Stop worrying your empty little head about Santa. No-one will miss him. (*To the audience*) You won't miss him, will you? Well, tough luck.

They exit to their Goblin Hollow

There is the sound of bolts and chains

Anna (*off*) Aaah.

Tommy (*off*) It's only a dead branch.

Anna, Tommy, Fergus and Prancer enter

Anna It was like a hand grabbing me.

Prancer You're lucky you don't have antlers. I thought I'd be knotted there for life.

Tommy Anyway, we've got here.

Fergus It looks a goblinly sort of place.

Anna It's horrible.

They take in the scene. No-one wants to be too far away from the others, though neither Fergus or Tommy would admit it

Prancer Do you feel as if we're being watched?

Anna By some thing that hates us.

Tommy Look at the light shining from the tree roots.

Anna It's so pale, like...

Tommy Like death light.

Prancer Let's come back when the sun's up.

He tries to exit, but Fergus is too quick

Fergus You stay here. (*To Tommy and Anna*) It's only the light from the Goblin Hollows.
Prancer That's meant to be a comfort, is it?
Fergus (*ignoring him*) See, every tree has a door. The light comes through the gaps round the frame. Now, beyond one of those doors is Santa. The question is, which one?
Tommy We could knock on each door in turn and ask them.
Fergus I wouldn't do that if I were you. If we start banging on all the doors it would only make the goblins angry. Then there'd be trouble.
Anna So what do we do?
Fergus Spread out and look out for clues.
Prancer Not likely!
Anna Must we?
Tommy There's nothing to be afraid of.

A bolt is slid back

What was that?
Fergus Come on, let's start.

Fergus exits

The others go the opposite way with great reluctance, keeping close together

Snottle opens the door, carrying a milk bottle

Prancer (*seeing Snottle*) Look out.

Anna, Tommy and Prancer duck for cover

Snottle What was that?

He looks about nervously. Every time he looks the other way, Anna, Tommy and Prancer crawl further away

Must be mice. (*He goes down stage and addresses the audience in a whisper)* I've got a message from Sneergripe, so you'd better listen. We heard some of you saying which way we'd gone. I told you not to do that, didn't I? We'll forgive you this time, but any more sneaking and there'll be big trouble. (*He backs towards the door*)

Fergus backs on stage looking up at the branches for clues. The two bump into each other

Snottle } (*together*) { Eaargh!
Fergus } { Aah! Have you seen Santa Claus anywhere?
Snottle You a policeman or something?
Fergus You could say I'm doing police work.
Snottle Ah. Well. No.
Fergus You sure?
Snottle No. I mean, yes. I didn't, I wasn't and I never. (*He tries to escape*)
Fergus (*restraining him*) Heard any suspicious sounds tonight?
Snottle Bags of them over there. (*He points to where the others are hid*) Fair put the willies up me.
Fergus (*to the others*) Come on, then. Where is he? (*He discovers who it is*) What are you doing down there?

Snottle bolts himself inside again, leaving the milk bottle outside with a note stuck in it

Prancer Looking for clues.
Anna Was that the kidnapper?
Fergus Of course it wasn't. Do you think I'd have let him go if it was? I hoped he might have seen something. Unfortunately, he hadn't.
Prancer Let's find someone who did, then.
Fergus Like who?
Owl (*off*) Who?
Fergus That's what I said. Who?
Owl (*off*) Twit.
Fergus No-one calls Fergus Lebrun a twit, least of all some antler-brained quadruped.
Owl (*off*) Who?
Fergus You, that's who! (*He threatens Prancer*)

Anna steps in the way

Anna Prancer didn't say anything.
Prancer That's right.
Anna None of us did.
Fergus Then who was it? There's no-one else here.
Prancer It's a ghost!

He rushes off, despite Fergus's attempt to stop him

Fergus I do wish Santa would use polar bears. They're so much more reliable.
Owl (*off*) And, I hope, much more polite.

Owl enters

Ghost indeed!
Anna It's an owl.
Owl Of course I'm an owl. I wouldn't be an ostrich, would I? (*He looks them over*) You have a problem.
Fergus We certainly do.
Owl I know, I know. I'm always right. Always.
Tommy (*to Anna*) My teacher keeps telling me no-one's right all the time. Not even me.
Owl What's that? Teachers? Not wise people at all. Very foolish, most of them. I know. I went to school once myself, you see. A very silly waste of my time it was, I can tell you. I knew everything already.
Fergus Then you can tell us who were the goblins that kidnapped Santa Claus, and where we can find them?
Owl Indeed I can.

There is a long pause

Fergus Well?
Owl You haven't asked me yet, have you? You only asked if I could tell you the answer. Well, I can. I can tell you lots of things—how far it is to the moon, how to boil an egg, how to say "I am a wise owl" in Mongolian and one hundred and forty-three other languages. But I won't tell you anything if you don't ask. I have my dignity, you know.
Fergus Now look here, my man——
Owl Bird.

Fergus My bird, I am Fergus Lebrun.

Owl You are also very rude.

Fergus What's that?

Owl Rude. R—U—D—E. It is not at all polite to assume I don't know something, to wit, your name.

Anna How do you know who we are?

Owl I don't. Why should I? My mind is an encyclopaedia, not a telephone directory.

Tommy Then you didn't know Fergus's name.

Owl No, but that's not the point.

Fergus He's worse than a reindeer.

Anna Mr Owl, please tell us where we can find the goblins who kidnapped Santa Claus.

Owl Would you like the answer in Chinese, Swahili, Serbo-Croat——

Anna English, please.

Owl What a dull little girl you are. But as you like. Try number seven—Sneergripe, Snottle and Bug.

Owl exits

Fergus Where's number seven then?

Tommy (*walking round the trees*) This one's number five.

Anna So this one is six.

Tommy No, that's nine. They're not in order.

Anna Here's number seven. The one with the milk bottle. (*She reads the note*) "One extra pint, please". That'll be for Santa.

Tommy That was the door the goblin went back in.

Fergus I wanted to lull him into a false sense of security.

Anna The door's locked. How do we get in?

Tommy We need a plan. Daring but cunning.

Fergus Exactly. Going at them like a bull at a gate won't get us anywhere. Stealth. That's the watchword. (*He marches up to the door and bangs on it loudly*)

Sound of bolts

Then Sneergripe opens the door

Sneergripe Please use the doorbell like everyone else.

He disappears again, shutting the door and replacing the bolts

Fergus thumps on the door, thinks better of it, and presses the bell instead

Sneergripe (*off*) This is the Sneergripe, Snottle and Bug residence. Please press the red button and speak into the microphone—now.
Tommy Fancy having an intercom on your front door when you live in a tree.
Fergus Open this door immediately.
Sneergripe (*off*) Do me a favour. Don't you know what time it is?
Fergus It's one-thirty-three in the morning. Now give me back Santa right away.
Sneergripe (*off*) Hang on.

After a pause, the locks are drawn back, and Sneergripe opens the door

Let's have the six million pounds then.
Fergus Don't be ridiculous. This is Christmas Eve, my man. I've no time to play games.
Sneergripe Push off.

He goes back in and shuts the door

Fergus (*alternately banging the door and ringing the bell*) Come back here this minute.

Sneergripe opens the door

Sneergripe Can't you read? Our ransom note clearly said——
Fergus I don't care a gnat's knee about your ransom note. I am Fergus Lebrun, Chief Forebrownie to his Jolliness Santa Claus. I want him back and I want him back now.
Sneergripe Get knotted! (*He tries to slam the door, but Fergus has his foot in the way*) Persistent wretch, aren't you?
Fergus Stop trying to kick me in the shins and listen. If I don't get Santa brought up to me right away, I'll fetch the police. What do you say to that, my lad?
Sneergripe Police? That's different. (*He shouts inside*) Bug! Snottle!
Fergus (*to Tommy and Anna*) Let them know who's boss, that's the secret.

Sneergripe I'll call them on the intercom, if I can just squeeze past.

Fergus does not move from the front door, so it is a tight squeeze

Bug! Snottle! Wake up. We have a Brownie here come to collect Santa.
Take him down to the guest-room please.
Snottle (*off*) Guest-room?
Sneergripe Where we put our guests, you fool.
Snottle Oh, the——
Sneergripe That's right.
Fergus I haven't got time to waste, you know.
Sneergripe It won't take a minute, I promise you. If the lady and the
gentleman would also like to come this way as well.
Anna We'll stay where we are.
Tommy Now don't be silly.
Anna Please, Tommy. That's even worse than here, and here's horrible.
Sneergripe As you like. A couple of kids can't do any harm. (*To Fergus*)
After you, sir.

*Fergus steps through the door, Sneergripe follows him, slamming the
door behind him*

There is a loud scream from Fergus, then silence

The door opens, Sneergripe picks up the milk bottle

Sneergripe Better make that two extra pints.

*He alters the note, replaces the bottle, and shuts the door. Again the
bolts are shut*

Tommy I don't think that was a good idea.
Anna What are we going to do now? We can't leave Fergus, but this
place... (*She shivers*) Tommy, let's run and get help while we've got the
chance.
Tommy You don't think anyone will believe us, do you? Reindeer,
goblins, talking dogs—not a hope! We have to do this ourselves.
Anna (*eagerly*) You've got a plan?
Tommy (*reluctantly*) No—but I will have, if only you'd keep quiet for
five minutes. (*He thinks*)

Anna becomes more and more anxious

Anna Tommy, it's not safe here. I know it's not.
Tommy Hush, I'm thinking.
Anna Mr Owl! Are you still there? Please tell us what we should do.

Owl enters

Owl Now there's an interesting question. First I must consider what you mean by the words "do" and "should". One must know first principles in order to make progress in any matter.
Anna (*desperately*) But we haven't got time.
Owl Then you should make time. Why I bother with such an impatient young lady I do not know, but if you insist on a quick answer, I suggest you seriously think about running for your lives. Good-night.

Owl exits

Tommy and Anna look round

Tommy What's he on about?
Anna Tommy!

Goblins creep on stage

Goblins We don't like kids who wake us up.

Tommy and Anna run to the other exit

More goblins appear there. They laugh and draw nearer

Just as the circle is about to join, Tommy sees a gap. He pulls Anna to it, dodging the outstretched goblin hands

Tommy and Anna exit while the goblins sort themselves out of their tangle

Goblin Leader Get after them.

The goblins exit in pursuit as——

——the CURTAIN *falls*

SCENE 4

A field near the forest

From the darkness there is the noise of goblins, shouting and whooping

Goblins (*off*) Bite 'em! Kick 'em! Whip 'em! Slash 'em!

Tommy and Anna enter from among the audience

Tommy Come on, Anna.
Anna Can't—run—more.
Tommy We're out of the wood now. Keep going and they won't follow us.

They run towards the stage

Anna Tommy—they're still coming after us.

The goblins come rushing in

Tommy We can still outrun them.

More goblins appear in front of them

Anna screams

This way. Quick.

A third group of goblins appear to block their escape

Back to back. We'll try to fight our way out.

The goblins close in

Goblin 1 Shall we boil them?
Goblin 2 Or mash them?
Goblin 3 Or tear them into little pieces?
Goblin Leader Or shall we do all three?
Anna Sorry, Tommy. If I'd listened to you, we'd both be tucked in bed now.
Tommy And if I'd listened to you, we'd have left Dead Man's Ditch
   before they were out of their Goblin Hollows.
Anna We'll do better next time, won't we.
Tommy Next time we'll work as a team.

Anna If there is a next time.

A goblin feigns an attack. Tommy shrinks back. Anna screams. The goblins laugh and try the new game again

Goblin Leader That's enough playing. Let's work them over in earnest.
Colonel (*off*) Flock, charge!

Colonel, Prancer and the sheep enter

For a moment there is a confusion of bodies and a lot of noise. When it clears, a ring of sheep protect Tommy, Anna, Prancer and Colonel from the goblins

Colonel My, you certainly made that lot angry.
Tommy Fergus woke them up banging on the kidnappers' door.
Colonel Rather foolish thing for him to do, if I may say so. And where is he now?
Anna He told the kidnappers to give Santa back, but they didn't. They kidnapped him instead.
Prancer He's so hasty. He means well, but one must say he's hasty.
Goblin Leader Right, me boyos. Two kids and a bunch of dumb animals. We'll sort them out in a couple of ticks. We'll have sheepskin coats each for Christmas. And a pair of childskin gloves.
Prancer They're about to attack.
Colonel Couldn't be better. Flock reform!

The goblins charge. Another mêlée, which ends with the goblins surrounded by a ring of sheep, with the others safely outside

Goblin Leader This is wrong. Let's get after them.
Sheep 1 Lay one claw on me and I'll bite.
Goblin Leader Don't listen. Sheep don't bite.
Goblin 1 You go first then.
Goblin Leader Softie! All you have to do is to give them a poke like this and——

Sheep 1 bites him. He screams

Goblin 1 Yeah, simple ain't it!

Goblin Leader If you don't want your face filled in, keep your trap shut.
Goblin 1 You and whose army?

Goblin Leader hits him. Goblin 1 retaliates. The other goblins join in

Colonel There's goblins for you. Tough as nails when their temper's up, but just as likely to fight themselves as anyone else.
Prancer What happens to us if they stop?
Colonel They won't do that. A goblin fight lasts for hours once it gets started. And when it's over, they'll be back to normal. Nasty and evil, but ready to run if they saw as much as a goldfish.
Anna Your sheep were magnificent.
Colonel Don't say that so loudly or else they'll be so conceited there'll be no controlling them. Between ourselves, though, they didn't do at all badly when it mattered. I'm really beginning to taste next year's prize bone already. But standing here gossiping won't do. We've got our own job to do.
Prancer He's going to rescue Santa for us—and Fergus as well, though I'm not sure he deserves it.
Anna Can you do it?
Colonel I won't pretend it's going to be easy. Irregular troops against a strongly defended position, you see. But a surprise stroke might pull it off.

Colonel and Prancer exit

Tommy I hope his surprise stroke is better than Fergus's stealth. I don't fancy Christmas in a goblin dungeon.
Anna It'll be all right. We're a team now, don't forget.

Tommy and Anna exit

Black-out

Scene 5

Sneergripe's Dungeon

On one side is a large cell containing Barbie, Fergus and Santa, the last two bound hand and foot. Santa is asleep. So is Bug, sitting in a rocking

*chair, snoring loudly. The room also has a table at the back, with some
empty packing cases marked "Grandma Grumble's Olde English Cabbage and Colde Porridge Cookies". There is also a microphone for the
door communication system*

Barbie It's quiet here at the moment.
Fergus I can't say I've noticed.
Barbie Shut up, Bug.

Bug stops snoring

Yes, not many of us here at the moment. They sent most prisoners home
for Christmas—save on Christmas dinner, you see. There's only us left.
Fergus Isn't there some way we can escape?
Barbie You don't want to do that. We're one big happy family down here,
aren't we, Bug? Just like the old days, though the company was better
then.
Fergus Thanks.
Barbie I dare say you want to hear about the old days.
Fergus As a matter of fact, I don't——
Barbie We can't have you disappointed, can we? I had hundreds of
visitors then. Princesses and knights most of them. The knights came to
rescue the princesses, you see. Ah, great days they were. Then my fire
went out. Of course, I went to see a firest—nice chap he was, except he
talked a lot—but he couldn't re-light it for me.
Fergus Firest, did you say?
Barbie I did. You see a dentist about your teeth, don't you? Well, dragons
see a firest about their fire. Now, where was I?
Fergus Near the end, I hope.
Barbie Ah yes, my fire. Without that no-one sent me princesses any more.
Fergus I should hope not. You should be ashamed of yourself, killing
those poor princesses.
Barbie (*horrified*) Killing!
Bug (*waking up*) Wozzat?
Barbie Go back to sleep, Bug, we're talking about fire.
Bug Oh, fire. Fire? Fire!

He runs out

Barbie I'll have you know I was a most respectable dragon. Any king would be pleased to have me look after his daughter. They'd stay with me for a week or two, until a knight came along to take them back. We'd have a battle for a couple of hours then a party afterwards. (*Confidentially*) I don't think any of the knights really wanted a princess, but it was their turn.

Bug rushes in with a fire bucket which he empties over what he hopes is the fire, but is actually Fergus

Fergus What? Oy!
Barbie Now, Bug, was that wise? Was that sensible?
Bug It put out the fire, didn't it?
Barbie (*to Fergus*) He's not very bright. (*To Bug*) Bug, I think the gentleman needs a towel. No, not your dirty hanky. A nice, clean dry towel.
Bug It was clean on last March.
Fergus I would prefer a towel.
Bug You get some fussy people down here.

Bug clanks off with the bucket

Barbie What was wrong with the princesses, that was what you were going to say, wasn't it?
Fergus Was it?
Barbie Dim, that's what. Not as dim as Bug, but—dim.
Fergus As it happens, I know some very clever——
Barbie No doubt you do, young man, but clever princesses don't sit in a dragon's cave for a week or two, not even if they have me for company. They get the stupid ones to do that. You know, I do enjoy talking to you. I hope you don't catch a fever from that soaking. I would be very disappointed if you died from it.
Fergus So would I. (*He tries to nod off during the following*)
Barbie I haven't had such a good talk since the old days. Pity about my fire, don't you think? You really need fire to fight knights. I tried using my claws but one does tend to fall over. It rather spoils the battle if you had to stop every five minutes to let one side get up. "Sorry, Barbie," the knights said, "have to cross you off the fixture list, old boy." And they did. Nobody came any more. I got very bored. And hungry. Oh yes, hungry. I couldn't cook anything, you see. Once I could spit roast an ox at twenty paces, but now... Lucky it had a happy ending, what?

Fergus (*waking up*) What?
Barbie Happy ending.
Fergus I don't see...
Barbie Of course you don't. Sneergripe kidnapped me. "If you don't tell me where your gold is, you'll stay here as prisoner," he said. So I didn't tell him. I stay here and let them do the cooking. Clever, eh?
Fergus Very.
Barbie Why hasn't Bug come back? I can't have him neglecting you. Bug!

Pause

Bug, get a move on!

Sneergripe enters

Sneergripe Can't you keep a bit of hush down here, Bug? Where's he gone?
Barbie To fetch my friend a towel.
Sneergripe Towel?
Barbie It's something that gentlemen—and ladies for that matter—dry themselves with. You wouldn't care to fetch one, would you?
Sneergripe No, I wouldn't.
Barbie (*to Fergus*) Sometimes the room service leaves a lot to be desired.
Sneergripe Room service! Don't you know the difference between a dungeon and a hotel?
Barbie Of course I do. You have to pay to stay in a hotel. Dungeons are free.
Sneergripe Look, Barbie, it's Christmas. Let's forget about the gold. Just go home, eh?
Barbie I wouldn't dream of going without telling you where to find my gold.
Sneergripe And about time too. Where is it, then?
Barbie I'm not telling you. I like it here. (*To Fergus*) I expect you'll like it after a year or two.
Sneergripe Get out!
Barbie Won't!
Santa (*waking up*) Do you mind? I'm trying to get some sleep.
Sneergripe This is my dungeon and I'll do what I like in it. And what I really would like at the moment is something particularly nasty to happen to you. Snottle!

Snottle comes running in

Ah, there you are. Do something slow, painful and agonising to the prisoners.
Barbie Really, what is this place coming to?
Sneergripe And make it extra painful for the dragon.

He stalks out

Fergus You've got us into a fine mess, haven't you?
Barbie It's all right. I won't fit on the rack and my scales are so hard they'll break the thumb screws.
Santa That'll be a lot of comfort when they put them on us.
Barbie I'll put in a kind word for you.
Santa Don't you dare.
Snottle Right, then. Where shall I begin?

The door bell rings

Barbie You might start by answering the door.
Snottle (*speaking into the microphone*) This is the Sneergripe, Snottle and Bug residence. Please press the red button and speak into the microphone—now.
Tommy (*off*) Good-evening. You wouldn't have seen a sick Brownie, would you?
Snottle No Brownies. (*He switches off*) Let's get back to breaking a bone or two. (*To Santa*) Might make you easier to carry, mayn't it?

The bells rings again

Snottle This is the Sneergripe, Snottle and——
Tommy (*off*) We've done that bit before. If you do happen to see that Brownie, keep away. He's very infectious.
Snottle Does that mean he's got a lot of money?
Tommy (*off*) No, it means he's got lots of diseases which you'll catch from him. Very rare and deadly diseases they are too. Yellow fever, scarlet fever, green monkey fever, blackwater fever, blue devil fever, pink——
Snottle He wouldn't look sort of—well, like a Brownie.
Tommy (*off*) That's him. Give us plenty of warning before you come to the door. You've probably caught something nasty already.

Snottle Bug, chuck that Brownie out of here.

Santa And me. I've caught them all as well.

Barbie People aren't as strong as they were in my day. It's television that does it.

Snottle Where's Bug gone?

Barbie Doesn't anyone ever listen? He's fetching a towel.

Santa We can always let ourselves out.

Snottle (*into the microphone*) I'll open the door and you can fetch him yourself.

Snottle exits

Barbie My cousin used to suffer from athlete's foot, you know. Very painful if you've got claws. He used to say to me, "Barbie——"

He is interrupted by the voices off stage

Snottle (*off*) Here, not so many.

Tommy (*off*) You can't expect two children to carry a heavy Brownie.

Snottle (*off*) He can walk.

There is a loud squawk, followed by alternate shouts of "Help" and cries of pain

> *Snottle tumbles on, with Prancer at his heels. Tommy, Anna and Colonel follow*

Tommy I told you reindeer had a kick like Gary Lineker.

Colonel (*to Prancer*) Sit on him if he doesn't behave.

Fergus I'm certainly glad to see you again, Colonel.

Colonel Let's get out again before being too cheerful. Where's the cell key?

Santa On his belt.

Anna There's the key. Here, Tommy, you're good with knots. (*She tosses him the key*)

He opens the cell and starts to untie Fergus

Colonel (*to Anna*) You watch this door. I'll watch the other.

> *Bug enters before they can take up position. He's carrying a mop*

Bug I couldn't find a towel. Will this do instead? What are you doing down there, Snottle?

Snottle What do you think I'm doing, playing sand castles?

Bug There isn't any sand. (*To Prancer*) Hallo, I'm Bug. Can I join in as well? Here, you're helping the prisoners escape. You can't play that game.

Colonel (*to Anna*) Keep under cover. I'll deal with him.

Anna takes refuge under the table. Colonel goes for Bug, but is forced back by the mop. Snottle takes his chance to escape

Snottle I'll get help.

Prancer You'll get thumped.

Snottle exits with Prancer in pursuit

Tommy I can't get these knots undone.

Santa There's a cutlass somewhere. Bug had it earlier.

Anna scrambles onto the table and Tommy leaves the cell as they hunt for the cutlass

Anna Over there, Tommy.

Tommy goes to fetch it. For a while, Bug alternately drives Colonel back with one stroke of the mop, and keeps Tommy away with the next. Eventually, Tommy gets hold of it. He hesitates over whether to free Fergus or help Colonel

Colonel Don't worry about me. Get Anna and the others out of here.

Anna Look out, Colonel.

Colonel is now getting the worst of Bug's concentrated attack. Tommy cuts Fergus free. Fergus rushes to help

Fergus Right, Goblin, I'll soon sort you out.

A well-aimed blow from Bug's mop leaves Fergus gasping on the floor

Bug (*to Colonel*) Give up yet?

Colonel Not likely.

Bug drives him back towards the table

Anna Stop! (*She tilts a box*)

Bug looks up, and she lets it fall over his head so that he can neither see nor move his arms. He staggers blindly round the dungeon during the ensuing exchanges

Colonel That saved all our bacon, ma'am.
Barbie A lot of excitement about nothing, if you ask me.
Santa Sorry, Barbie, we've got to go now.

Sneergripe enters with the blunderbuss

Sneergripe On the contrary. You will all be staying a little longer.
Santa It's Sneergripe.
Sneergripe Indeed it is. For the benefit of those of you who have yet to make my acquaintance, I am by profession a master criminal and evil genius. I am also very angry at the disturbance you are causing my happy little household. (*Threateningly*) Now into that cell and quick. (*He herds everyone back into*
the cell)
Tommy Cheer up, Colonel. It nearly worked.
Colonel Nearly isn't good enough. We're in trouble now.
Sneergripe Indeed you are.
Anna What are you going to do with us?
Sneergripe I don't know yet, but whatever it is, you won't like it one little bit. (*To Tommy*) Little boys don't play with cutlasses, so hand over.

Tommy hands the cutlass over

That's right. Now be sure and make friends with your fellow prisoners. It's so nice to have friends at one's funeral.

He is about to lock the cell door when Bug, still trapped in the box, barges into him. As Sneergripe tries to rise, Fergus pushes the cell door open. Sneergripe goes for the gun and Fergus for the cutlass

Tommy Watch his gun.

Fergus No, you don't.

Fergus blocks Sneergripe. Sneergripe knocks him aside, but Colonel pulls him back. By the time he breaks free, Tommy has the gun

Tommy How does it work?
Fergus (*picking up the cutlass*) I know how this works.
Sneergripe Bug! Snottle! Smash them.

Bug rushes towards the voice. He misses everyone, continues into the cell and falls over Barbie

Barbie (*removing the box*) See what happens if you run round with a box on your head.
Bug I thought it got dark early.
Santa Your turn for the cells, Sneergripe.
Sneergripe We shall see who laughs last.

Prancer enters, pushing Snottle

Prancer It won't be this obnoxious little object.
Sneergripe Snottle, I am ashamed of you. Here was your chance to rescue your beloved leader, and what do you do? Fail me.
Snottle Sorry, Sneergripe.
Sneergripe You certainly will be.

Snottle and Sneergripe join Bug in the cell. The others leave it

Santa What you might call a perfect ending.
Barbie I don't know about that. I was perfectly happy where I was.
Fergus No-one's making you leave.
Barbie In that case, I should be locked up. Rules and rules.

Tommy locks Barbie in

Santa Now listen carefully, Barbie. You only let those goblins out one at a time to cook meals, scrub floors and do anything else you're too lazy to do yourself. And if I find Sneergripe on the loose, I'll come back and rescue you properly.

Fergus Why not tell them your life story as well—at least twice a day. They deserve it.

Bug I like a good story.

Sneergripe Shut up, Bug.

Barbie Be quiet, Sneergripe. I'm in charge here.

Fergus I don't want to spoil the party.

Santa But we have five hundred seventy-three million, one hundred seventy-six thousand, four hundred and ninety-two toys to deliver in—how long, Fergus?

Fergus Four hours, three minutes and twenty-two seconds.

Santa We're going to need some help this year, aren't we, Fergus? As our friends are so resourceful, perhaps they'd be willing to lend a hand?

Tommy Delighted.

Colonel Honoured.

Anna Oh, can I?

Santa Bring them along, then. And whistle up the team, Prancer.

Prancer exits

It doesn't take very long to learn how to walk through a wall carrying a sack of toys. The knack is, don't try it where there's a bit of furniture in the way.

Santa, Fergus, Tommy, Anna and Colonel exit

Barbie settles down in the rocking chair

Barbie Now we can have a bit of peace, maybe.

Bug Did Santa leave me my train set?

Barbie You'll have to wait until morning to find that out.

Bug Let's sing carols while we wait. (*He starts to sing loudly and out of tune*)

Sneergripe Shut up, Bug.

Barbie I like a nice singsong. Keep going, Bug.

Bug continues, to the delight of Barbie and the agony of the others

CURTAIN

EPILOGUE

Near Tommy and Anna's House

Santa, Fergus, Colonel, Tommy and Anna enter

Tommy has Fergus's list; Anna has three sacks

Fergus Thank goodness that's over. It's bad enough delivering toys at the best of times, but with goblins as well—it's too much at my age.

Santa Is that the lot?

Tommy We've everything ticked off from Aardvarksdorp——

Santa We don't mention Aardvarksdorp, do we Fergus?

Tommy —to Zweinberg-oder-Pigg.

Anna But there's three sacks left.

Tommy We loaded too many on the last trip.

Santa Fergus would never let us do that.

Fergus Not likely.

Anna (*opening a sack*) This one's got nothing but bones in it.

Santa What else would you give a sheep dog but a year's supply of bones?

Colonel Don't think I'm ungrateful, but...

Santa Something for the sheep as well? It's under the bones.

Anna (*opening the next sack*) This one is full of books. The *En-cy-clo-paed-ia.*

Tommy *Britannica.*

Santa De Luxe edition in Burgundy calf with gold tooling.

Tommy Wasn't I getting that anyway?

Fergus No, football boots.

Tommy Boots and the encyclopaedia! Couldn't be better.

Anna (*opening the last sack*) This one's... Oh!

Santa (*to Fergus*) I told you it was what she's always wanted.

Colonel Thank you for the bones, Santa, but I must be getting back now. What do you think my farmer would say if he found he'd been given a pack of goblins for Christmas?

Santa (*to Tommy and Anna*) And you should be in bed, otherwise you won't be in time to wake up on Christmas morning.

Anna Can we help again next year?

Santa If I get kidnapped by goblins you can. Goodbye.

As they wish each other goodbye and Merry Christmas——

> *——the* CURTAIN *opens to show the rest of the cast ready for the curtain call*

FURNITURE AND PROPERTY LIST

Further dressing may be added at the director's discretion

PROLOGUE

Off stage: Boxes (**Brownies**)
Extremely long list (**Fergus**)
Sleigh (**Reindeer**)

Personal: **Brownie:** piece of paper
Reindeer: bells

SCENE 1

On stage: Dustbin

Off stage: Shoe (**Stage Management**)
Tennis ball (**Bug**)
Large box. *In it:* 24 packets of cabbage and cold porridge cookies
  (**Bug**)
Notice (**Sneergripe**)

Personal: **Reindeer:** bells
Snottle: gagging rags
Prancer: whistle

SCENE 2

On stage: Gate
2 stiles

Off stage: Box. *In it:* **Santa** (**Snottle and Bug**)

Personal: **Bug:** football comic
Granny Rabbit: carrots
Prancer: bells

Scene 3

Off stage:	Box (Snottle and Bug) Milk bottle. *In it:* note (Sneergripe)
Personal:	**Sneergripe:** sheets of paper, notepaper **Prancer:** bells

Scene 4

Personal:	**Prancer:** bells

Scene 5

On stage:	Rocking chair Boxes Microphone Cutlass
Off stage:	Fire bucket (**Bug**) Blunderbuss (**Sneergripe**) Mop (**Bug**)
Personal:	**Prancer:** bells **Bug:** handkerchief

Epilogue

Off stage:	**Fergus's** list (**Tommy**) 3 sacks. *In them:* bones, *Encyclopaedia Britannica*, football boots (**Anna**)

LIGHTING PLOT

Property fittings required: nil
Various interior and exterior settings

PROLOGUE
To open: Overall night-time lighting

No cues

SCENE 1
To open: Overall night-time lighting

Cue 1   As everyone exits   (Page   16)
            Fade lights out

SCENE 2
To open: Overall night-time lighting

No cues

SCENE 3
To open: Overall night-time lighting

No cues

SCENE 4
To open: Overall night-time lighting

Cue 2   **Tommy** and **Anna** exit   (Page   40)
            Fade to black-out

SCENE 5
To open: Overall night-time lighting

No cues

EPILOGUE
To open: Overall night-time lighting

No cues

EFFECTS PLOT

Lightning Source UK Ltd.
Milton Keynes UK
UKHW021252160721
387272UK00007B/58